ABRAC

Magic an

You too can be a magician! And who better to teach you
the tricks of the trade than star performer Shari Lewis!
ABRACADABRA! is stuffed with all sorts of terrific
tricks – and none of them calls for any equipment. You'll
be amazed to discover that all the props you need are
already in your home. You'll only need your wits! Learn
tricks with coins, cards, calculators and codes! Perform
pranks with paper, pencils and parts of the body!
Master magic with maths, matchsticks, messages and
mind-reading! In no time at all, you will be astounding
your family and friends with your expertise. All it takes
is this book – and a little bit of practice.

One of America's most talented and popular TV
personalities, Shari Lewis is probably best-known as
sidekick to Lamb Chop, the wisecracking hand-puppet.
But she has also written twenty-two books, has made
many record albums and is a renowned symphony
orchestra conductor. *ABRACADABRA!* is Shari
Lewis's first book to be published in Puffin.

Shari Lewis

ABRACADABRA!
Magic and Other Tricks

Illustrated by Mike Gordon

PUFFIN BOOKS

Puffin Books, Penguin Books Ltd, Harmondsworth, Middlesex, England
Viking Penguin Inc., 40 West 23rd Street, New York, New York 10010, U.S.A.
Penguin Books Australia Ltd, Ringwood, Victoria, Australia
Penguin Books Canada Ltd, 2801 John Street, Markham, Ontario, Canada L3R 1B4
Penguin Books (N.Z.) Ltd, 182–190 Wairau Road, Auckland 10, New Zealand

First published by World Almanac Publications, New York, 1984
Published in Puffin Books 1985

Made and printed in Great Britain by
Cox & Wyman Ltd, Reading
Typeset in 12/15 pt Palatino by
Rowland Phototypesetting Ltd
Bury St Edmunds, Suffolk

☆ TABLE OF CONTENTS ☆

To my favourite mother, Ann Ritz Hurwitz, who
has never stopped growing.

Acknowledgements to consultants Leo Behnke and adviser Dr A. B. Hurwitz (formerly Peter Pan The Magic Man, official magician for the City of New York, otherwise known as Daddy).

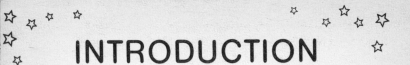

INTRODUCTION

Did you ever hear the joke about the magician who called the girl up on stage to be his assistant? To prove to the audience that this girl was not his partner, he said, 'Now, you've never seen me before, have you?' And the girl answered, 'No, Daddy.'

That's the story of my life. My father was a magician. His stage name was 'Peter Pan the Magic Man', and for twenty-eight years he was the official magician of the City of New York. Ever since I can remember, my father was pulling rabbits out of hats and making coins drop out of my friends' ears. That's really how I got into the business of performing.

This book is full of terrific tricks, some of them taught to me by my father. To do these tricks you don't need a magician's top hat, cape or magic wand. You can pretend you're doing them on the spur of the moment. You don't need fancy equipment – you probably have everything you need in the house. If the magic bug bites you and you want to explore other tricks, you can find lots of great equipment at magic shops. But for now, this book is your starter set.

Before you begin, here are just three tricky tips:

First, sometimes when I'm reading instructions I have trouble understanding what they mean. I find that the best thing to do is to read on. The next sentence often tells me the next move, which helps me to understand the hard part.

Second, lots of tricks that seem to be done on the spur of the moment actually take a bit of preparation. I often set up a trick and keep it ready in my desk or my pocket long before I want to perform it, the same way some people save up jokes to use in their conversation.

Third, as I'm performing a trick, I never tell my audience what I'm going to do before I do it. That way if I make a mistake it won't be tragic, since the audience doesn't know what I meant to do. Besides, a good trick is like a good joke – it takes you by surprise.

I hope this book helps you discover that you have the magic touch! Ready? Set? Abracadabra!

DO YOU HAVE THE MAGIC TOUCH?

Mealtime Miracle

You put a cup, fork, spoon and saucer on the table in that order, going from left to right. You tell your friend to choose any one of the objects mentally, but not to tell you which was picked. Then, as you tap the objects with a pencil, your friend is to *spell the name of the object silently*, one letter to each tap, and say 'Stop' at the last letter. Your pencil will be resting on the very object that your friend secretly picked. (For example, if the cup was chosen, your friend would think C on the first tap, U on the second, and your pencil would be pointing to the cup as your friend got to think P.)

Here's how it works: the objects are spelt with three, four, five or six letters. (Cup is three, fork is four, spoon is five, saucer is six.) You make the first two taps on any object. You then go from left to right, tapping each object once. As the last letter is silently spelt by your friend, you will be tapping the object he or she picked. So if the word was CUP, the C and U would be tapped anywhere, but on P you'd have gone to the object on the left, which is the cup.

The New Shell Game

Here's how you can play the shell game as a game or as a trick.

Start with three paper cups and one biscuit. Place the biscuit under one of the cups and switch the cups around so that your friends can't tell which cup the biscuit is under. The game is this: whoever guesses where the biscuit is keeps it.

That'll be fun for your friends, but here's the way you can make it *magic* and even more fun.

Beforehand, glue a single hair from your head to the rim of one cup. The hair, which no one else will see, will make it possible for you to keep your eye on that cup. Place the biscuit under it and then let your friends rearrange all the cups as quickly as they can, trying to confuse you. You will always be able to tell exactly where that biscuit is.

The Sticky Solution

Do your parents complain that you make money disappear faster than they can earn it? Would you like to show them that you can magically change four coins into five? That'll keep them quiet!

Here's how it works: before you do this trick, hide a coin under the edge of a table. Stick it there with a bit of soap, a tiny blob of chewing gum, or a drop of rubber cement.

When your parents are ready, roll up your sleeves and place four coins on the table. Now cup your right hand just below the table. With your left hand, brush the four coins into your right hand and close it.

Now ask Mum and Dad to blow on your hand. Then slowly open your fingers and show five coins instead of four!

The secret is simple. As the coins were being pushed into your right hand, the fingers of that hand were reaching under the table and picking up the hidden coin.

Tell Mum and Dad that money made in this way doesn't even have to be declared on the family's income tax.

Sum Trick!

Ask your friend to write down any two numbers, one under the other. Then ask him or her to add these two numbers together, and put the sum under them. Say, 'Continue to add the sum of the last two numbers and write that sum under the other numbers. Keep on doing this until there are ten numbers in the column.' (On my list of numbers I have 1 and 5, which equals 6. Then I add the 5 and 6, which comes to 11. The 6 and 11 make 17, and so on.)

Now tell your friend, 'Add up the column of ten numbers as fast as you can.' The surprising thing is that before your friend gets very far, you'll know the answer. Can you work out how you'll do this?

Here's how: just multiply the *seventh number* in the row by 11, and you will get the sum of ten numbers, no matter what those numbers are!

And here's the shortest short cut to multiplying low two-digit numbers by 11: just add the two digits together, and put the sum in the middle. (So, to multiply 45 by 11, I added the 4 and the 5, and put the 9 in the middle, to get 495.) See page 112 to find a short cut for multiplying two high-digit numbers by 11.

Pick a Number

1	2	4	8
7	6	13	10
5	3	15	14
3	15	7	13
11	7	6	15
9	10	5	12
13	14	12	11
15	11	14	9

Copy this box full of numbers on to a 3 × 5 card or piece of paper and take it to school with you. You'll be able to do one of the best number tricks I have ever seen.

Say to a friend, 'Think of any number on this chart. Tell me which vertical (up and down) rows you find it in. If you find it in more than one row, tell me that, too, and I will tell you the number you thought of.'

Here's how you do it: memorize the numbers at the top of each vertical column (there are four of them – 1, 2, 4 and 8). When your friend tells you the rows the selected number is in, add all the top numbers in those rows. For example, if your friend picked 5, 5 is found in the first and third rows. The number at the top of the first row is 1, the number at the top of the third row is 4. You add 1 and 4 and you get 5, which is the number that your friend thought of.

OK – here's one more example. The number 15 is in all four rows. So you add up the four numbers at the top of the four rows: 1 + 2 + 4 + 8 – and you get 15. Good, eh?

Concentration

Say to a friend, 'This trick takes concentration. First, think of a number. Double it (I'll wait). Add 10. Divide the total that you get by 2. Now subtract the number you started with. Your answer will be 5.'

Your answer will always be 5, no matter what number you think of first. For example, if you started by thinking of the number 2, here's what you get:

$$2 + 2 = 4$$
$$4 + 10 = 14$$
$$14 \div 2 = 7$$
$$7 - 2 = 5$$

Try this trick on your friends. They'll be amazed. Are you amazed? Here's the simple, not-so-amazing-if-you-know-the-secret reason why the answer will always be 5: After you think of a number and double it, the number that you add can be any *even* number. The answer to the trick will always be *half* of that even number. (We added 10, so the answer had to be 5.)

For example, you could add 20 instead, and then the trick would run like this (let's start with the number 3, just for the fun of it):

$$3 + 3 = 6$$
$$6 + 20 = 26$$
$$26 \div 2 = 13$$
$$13 - 3 = 10$$

If you do this trick over and over for your friends, you can really confuse them by *picking a different even number to add every time.*

Pick the Date

Remember this one the next time you have a calendar handy. Ask your friend to pick any seven-day row of numbers on the calendar. Say, 'I'll add up the sum of that week of dates faster than you can!' On the word 'go', all you do is take the lowest number in that row and add three to it. Then multiply the answer you get by seven. You'll have the sum of those seven dates faster than your friend, unless he or she's a whiz. For example, if, say, the second week in January starts with the number 7, 7 plus 3 equals 10, and 10 times 7 equals 70. And if you add up the dates of that week, 7, 8, 9, 10, 11, 12, 13, you get 70.

JANUARY				1985		
1	2	3	4	5	6	7
8	9	10	11	12	13	14
15	16	17	18	19	20	21
22	23	24	25	26	27	28
29	30	31				

The Magic Finger

Here's a trick that may convince your friends you are magical right to your fingertips.

Cut a drinking-straw in half and put one of the halves on a table in front of you. Say, 'I'll magnetize the straw by drawing a circle around it with my pointer finger, and as I move that finger away the straw will follow it.' Yes, it will – because here's the secret: draw the circle around the straw with your finger. Do it three times. Lower your head as you do, watching the straw closely and positioning your head about twelve inches from the straw. Hold your lips slightly apart. After you circle, move your finger away from you and, at that moment, gently blow on the straw so that it follows your finger. Just make sure that your lips don't move as you blow. And for goodness' sake, blow without making any noise.

The Talking Card

Since I'm a ventriloquist, people think I can make anything talk. Here's a card trick that will give you a reputation as a ventriloquist as well as a magician, because the cards will talk to you.

Before you start, sneak a look at the top card of your pack. Then shuffle, keeping that top card on the top. Put the pack on your left hand and hold your right hand out, palm up. Tell your friend to cut the pack in half, placing the other half on your right hand. (You now have the top half of the pack on your right, the bottom half on your left.)

Tell your friend to take any card. If your friend takes the top card from the pile on your right hand, you can name it. (Why not? After all, it is the same card that was on the top of the pack, and you *memorized* that one.)

If your friend takes any other card in the entire pack (from either pile), tell him or her to touch that chosen card to the top of the pile in your right hand, and then to put the card to your ear. It is absolutely amazing, but the card your friend chose is going to tell you the name of the top card in that pile.

And when your friend turns over that top card and sees that you've guessed it correctly, don't forget to say 'thank you' to the card that 'talked' and helped you do the trick.

An Eye at the End of Your Finger

Say to someone, 'You can't tell, but I have an eye at the end of my finger.' Give the person a pack of cards to shuffle. Take them back and put them in your pocket . Then, by the sense of touch alone, call out the name of each card, one at a time, *before* you take it out of your pocket and show it.

Here's how: before you do this trick, take five cards from the pack, *memorize the order in which you're holding them*, and put them in your pocket in that order. (Don't let anyone see you do this!)

When the time comes to do your show, take the pack back from the person who shuffled it and put it in your pocket so that it's right under the five cards which you already have in your pocket. Then reach in, name the top card (which you have memorized), and take it out and show it to everyone. You can repeat this with the next four.

If you don't stop after five cards, your fingers are on their own!

Flap, Flap

This is an absolutely amazing trick, and if you don't tell anyone, no one will know that it's so.

Shuffle a pack of cards, then ask your friend to count any number of cards from the top of the pack face down into a pile on the table. Tell your friend to count the same number of cards into a second pile. (So let's say your friend counted ten cards down into the first pile. He or she would then have counted ten cards into the second pile as well.)

Put the rest of the pack aside for the duration of this trick.

Now say, 'Cut either pile to any card, remember the bottom card that you've cut to, and put the group of cards in your hand on top of the *other* pile. Now put the rest of the cards from the

20

first pile on top of the second pile as well.' In other words, let's pretend that your friend cut the first pile to the third card. (And we'll pretend that the third card was the ace of hearts.) Your friend would have memorized that card. Then those three cards would not have been put back on the first pile (from which they came) but rather on to the other pile. In addition, your friend would now pick up all the rest of that first pile and put those cards on top of the other pile, as well. Got it?

At this point, you, the magician, turn the cards over one at a time, and when you get to the card picked and memorized by your friend, you know exactly which it is.

Here's how you do it: secretly, when your friend counts the first group of cards into a pile, you listen to the cards flapping on to the table and remember how many cards were put down into that pile. And at the very end of the trick, when you have the pack in front of you, you simply count down that number of cards, and the card your friend selected will be at that number. (Remember, we pretended that your friend had counted down ten cards, and then cut to the ace of hearts? In that case, at the end of the trick, the tenth card would be the ace of hearts.)

Free Choice

I'm going to show you how to do a fine trick for two friends, and I guarantee that it'll work every time, but I'll be darned if I know why.

Put a 5p piece and a 1p piece on a table. Say to your friends, 'I'm going out of the room. While I'm out, one of you decide to be a liar, and when I come back, *only tell lies*. The other of you is *only to tell the truth*. And while I'm out, you have a free choice. Each one of you pick up one of the coins – whichever you choose – and hold it tightly in your hand.'

And then you, the magician, go out of the room, and your friends decide who is the liar and who is the truth-teller, and they each pick up one coin.

When you come back, point out to your two friends that they had a free choice of choosing to be a liar or a truth-teller. They also had the free choice of choosing either coin. Now you give them another choice. 'I'm going to ask one question. You tell me who to ask.'

Your friends will decide. Then you say to the one they've chosen, 'Did the liar take the 1p piece?' (That's exactly what you must say.)

Here's the funny part of this trick. If the person you asked says, 'Yes,' then the other person has the 1p piece. But if the person you asked says, 'No', then he or she has the 1p piece.

The Dancing Coin

I've heard of having to 'scratch out a living', but having to 'scratch for 20 pence' sounds sad, doesn't it? Not in this case! If you'll scratch for this 20p piece, it'll walk out from under a glass.

Here's how it works: on a table covered with a tablecloth, get someone to put down two 10p pieces. Ask that someone to place a 20p piece in between. Now position the 10p pieces so that the rim of a 'bottoms-up' glass sits right on them.

Then say, 'If I can get the 20p piece out from under that glass without touching the glass, can I keep it? If I can't do it, I'll give you 20 pence of my own!'

Your friend will probably think that's a good bet.

Then you simply scratch like a dog trying to get a bone. Scratch that tablecloth *towards* you and the 20p piece will dance right out from under the glass and into your pocket!

PICK A PET

What Happens

You show a list with lots of animal names on it, and a paper clip. You also have a little pack of cards. On each card is the name of one of the animals. Removing one card from the pack, you lay it face down on the table so that no one can read the name.

Now you slip the paper clip on to the edge of the sheet near the list, and slide the clip down the list of names, telling your friends to stop you anytime they wish. You turn the list round and show that the paper clip is circling the name of one of the animals. And when the card on the table is turned over, on it is that very same name!

How It Happens

Prepare your paper clip ahead of time. Better still, make up *three* of them. Below, you'll see three names in small rectangles (picture A). Copy these on to a sheet of plain paper, cut them out, and glue each one to a paper clip as shown in picture B. When the glue has dried, carefully trim off all the outside edges of the paper.

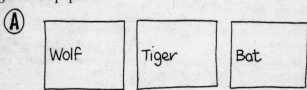

24

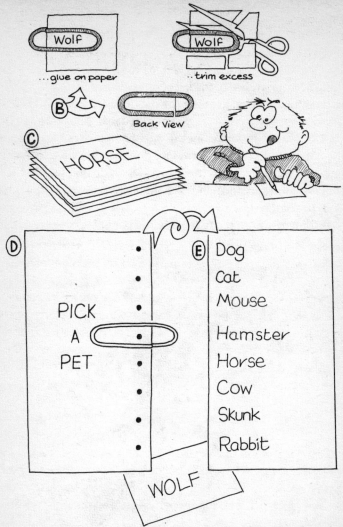

...glue on paper

...trim excess

B

Back View

C

HORSE

D

PICK
A
PET

E Dog
Cat
Mouse
Hamster
Horse
Cow
Skunk
Rabbit

WOLF

When you've done this, write out the following animal names on to pieces of card: DOG, COW, HORSE, TIGER, SKUNK, RABBIT, WOLF, BAT. You now have your little pack of animal cards (picture C). Then copy out another list of names on to a sheet of paper (E). On the reverse, draw a dot level with each animal name, and write PICK A PET (D).

When you're going to show someone the trick, put the list, the pack and one of the gimmicked paper clips together. Oh yes, *remember which name is glued to the paper clip*!

Show your audience the list of animals and the pack of cards with animal names, keeping the paper clip in your hand so no one can see that a piece of paper is glued to it. Look through the pack of names and take out the one that matches the name on the paper clip. Place that card face down on the table so that no one can read it. Hold up the list with the side that says PICK A PET to your audience and slip the paper clip on to the edge with the names (picture D).

Tell them you're going to slide the paper clip down the list. When it is opposite any one of the dots on their side, they

should tell you to stop. When they do this, *square up the edge of the list with the edge of the paper glued to the clip* so that they're even.

Turn the list round. Show your friends that they stopped you (apparently) at the name of a – (here you read the name *on the paper clip*). Ask your friends to turn over the card on the table, and they'll be surprised to see that the name on the card is the same.

As you slide the paper clip down the edge of the list, make sure there isn't a light *behind* you. If there is, your audience will see the shadow of the paper glued to the clip.

Don't do this trick twice for the same people during the same show. You've got the two *extra* names on two other paper clips, so you can repeat the trick at your *next* show without using the same animal, but *do* wait until the *next* show!

ARE YOU CRAFTY?

You don't have to be an expert at crafts to do these stunts. Most are pranks that just need a little something prepared ahead of time. In one case, all you have to do is make sure that you have a couple of pieces of paper and a pair of scissors handy.

A Ghost in Your Pocket

How would you like to pull out your pocket, make a spooky move, and have your pocket return into your trousers all by itself?

Here's how: knot one end of a thread. Stick it inside one pocket, through the trousers, to the inside of the other pocket. The knot will be on the inside of the first pocket, the rest of the thread will be loose inside the second pocket.

To do the trick, put in your hand and pull out the first pocket (the one with the knot in it). Show it empty and then make a few spooky moves above it. With your other hand (which is casually held in your other pocket) secretly pull in the thread. It will slowly tug that first pocket back into your trousers in a weird way.

A Snappy Trick

Next time you come across a handkerchief or a cloth napkin with a hem, treasure it!

When no one is watching, push a toothpick into the hem of that hanky or napkin. Later, when you have an audience, pick up a toothpick and ask someone to break it. But before they actually break it, say, 'Let me fold the toothpick into the handkerchief so no splinters will get into your palm.' Fold the cloth so that the toothpick your friend actually snaps is the one pushed into the hem.

And when you open the handkerchief, your audience will

see the whole toothpick lying there, unbroken and in perfect shape!

It really is a snappy trick – just don't try to do it twice in a row.

Just One Cut

Here's a stumper that I've never seen before. Now I'm not saying, 'I've seen them all,' but you should see my collection!

You can do this with your friends at school, using a piece of paper from your notebook, and instead of cutting the paper with scissors, you can tear it.

The challenge is this: how, with just one cut, can you divide a sheet of paper into three equal pieces?

Answer: fold the paper in half. Then fold that doubled sheet of paper into three even sections (see picture). If you make one cut – cutting off the section nearest to the fold (and cutting through the doubled sheet) – you will find that when you unfold the little section you have cut off, it will be exactly equal to the two other pieces.

PRANKS WITH A PARTNER

Sharing a secret is even more fun than keeping it to yourself – as long as you share it with a good friend. And your pranks will seem even more miraculous if nobody knows that you have a partner working with you!

Super Sleuth

How would you like to be able to solve a murder mystery, just like Sherlock Holmes?

What will happen: while you are out of the room, somebody will pick up an object and, with great melodrama, use it as a 'weapon' to pretend to 'murder' one of the other people in the room.

Then the 'murderer' will hide the 'weapon' on any one of the other innocent bystanders and take a seat to 'hide out'. You, the super sleuth, will come back into the room and, without asking any questions, find the weapon, identify the victim, and correctly point to the perpetrator of the crime. (The sillier the weapon, the greater the fun. Being shot by a key or stabbed by a pillow is real melodrama.)

How it works: one of the innocent bystanders is your secret confederate. (Of course, he or she must avoid being the murderer or the victim!) All this friend has to do is imitate the positions first of the victim and then of the criminal, and point to where the weapon is hidden – in that order.

So as you are being brought back into the room, your secret

31

friend takes on the same position as the victim (if his or her legs are crossed, so are your friend's, and so on).

Ten seconds later your confederate changes position to match that of the murderer. After another ten seconds, your friend duplicates the way the person hiding the weapon is positioned. A final shift of the hand shows where on that person the weapon can be found.

All of this is done as you wander around the room looking into people's faces and mumbling to yourself like any good detective. Finally, when you've got all the information, with one swoop you produce the weapon, identify the victim, and accuse the murderer.

Good Vibes

Oh, the groans, oh, the scorn – when I finally tell how my daughter and I do this trick. But until I tell, we get nothing but oohs and aahs.

Here's what we do: I leave the room and my daughter asks someone to pick a favourite number. Then somebody else brings me back into the room. At this point, I claim that my daughter and I have close communication, and her mental vibrations will tell me the number chosen in my absence. I put my fingertips lightly on her temple and, in a moment, I name the number.

Here's how I know: as I put my fingertips on the side of her head (supposedly to get her mental vibrations) she simply tightens her jaws. This makes the muscle under my fingers press out against them. She bites her teeth together once for each number. For example, if the number is 26, she would bite her teeth together twice (indicating 2), and then she would pause and bite her teeth together six times. That's 26. She and I have worked out a code for zero: she doesn't press her teeth together and lets her jaw go slack.

Sneaky Signals

Here's a trick for you and a friend to do at your next party. It'll knock 'em out at school, too. But no one must know that your friend is in on it.

What will happen: you go out of the room, and the rest of the group picks some object in plain view of everyone. You return and various things around the room are named, one after another. When the right object is named you say instantly, 'That's the one that was picked.'

How does your assistant indicate the object to you? He or she doesn't. The secret of this very baffling mystery is that *you* are the one who signals. Read on.

The trick: you come back into the room and your friend starts naming or pointing to objects in different parts of the room. Four, five or six objects are named and *when you want the selected object to be named you do something to change your position*: fold or unfold your arms, shift one foot, put your hands behind you, or any other natural and subtle movement. As soon as your assistant sees you do this, the next object he or she names must be the selected one. As soon as it is called, you announce that it was the group's choice.

Just this once, let yourself be pressured into doing the same trick twice, as the fun and frustration grow. The secret of this particular while-I'm-out-of-the-room trick is that everyone is watching and listening to your assistant, waiting for a signal that will never come.

The Word Wizard

In this bit of magic, you go out of the room. Your friend asks the rest of the group to think of a word. Let's suppose they decide on the word 'dog'.

Now you are called back into the room and in a little while you guess the selected word.

Here's how it works: when you come back into the room your friend will say, 'Do you know the word?' You hear that the first word he said started with the letter D, and so you know that the word you have to guess starts with a D too. You mumble, 'No,' (or whatever your favourite mumble is) and your friend says, 'Oh, come on, you can do it!' Now you know that the O is the second letter. When your friend urges you to 'Go on, have a guess,' you've got the final clue, G, and you can brighten up and say, 'Yes, yes, my magic powers are working – the word you selected was dog.'

Arrange with the person cueing you that when the word is finished, your friend will turn his or her back on you or sit down or do some other action to let you know that that's the last letter of the word.

Very easy code! Very good trick!

A Coin in a Cup

I wish I could show you this bit of magic before I tell you how it's done. Because it's so simple, you'll never believe how startling the illusion is.

You place a paper cup upside down on a table. You send your assistant out of the room and ask someone from the audience to hide a coin under the cup. You give the person from the audience a choice of four coins – a 1p, 2p, 5p or 10p coin. When the coin is hidden, you call your assistant back into the room. Your assistant immediately tells the audience which of the four coins is hidden under the cup.

Here's how it's done: somewhere on the side of the paper cup, you have made a tiny dot with a pencil or felt-tipped pen. When your assistant comes back, he or she simply looks for the dot. If it is facing your assistant, there is a 1p piece hidden under the cup. If the dot is to your assistant's right, there's a 2p piece under the cup. If the dot is to the assistant's left, a 5p piece is hidden. And if he or she cannot see the dot (because you've turned it away from your assistant and towards the audience) the 10p piece has been hidden.

HIGH SIGNS

There are lots of really good mind-reading tricks that can only be done if you and a friend know how to signal to each other without letting the audience know what's going on.

Here are four tricks. For most of them, you'll need a good friend as a partner. The two of you learn the tricks together. Then you can do them at parties or club meetings or in your classroom. For the last trick, you won't need a partner because you can get someone in the group to be your volunteer.

How can you and your partner signal to each other so that it looks as though you're reading each other's mind? Simple. You use hush-hush communications!

A Ten-Card Layout Trick

Here's what happens: a pack of cards is shuffled. Ten cards are taken from the pack and placed face up on the floor or a table.

Your partner goes out of the room so that he or she can't see or hear what's happening. Someone points to any one of the cards.

Now your partner is called back into the room. You start pointing to and calling out the names of the cards on the floor, one after another. When you call out the chosen card, your partner says, '*That's* the one that was picked!'

Here's how you do it: place a ten – the ten of clubs, hearts, spades or diamonds – on top of the pack. Let's say it's the ten of clubs, OK? As you shuffle, mix up all the rest of the cards, but keep putting the top few cards back on top, so the ten of clubs never leaves the top.

As you deal out ten cards from the top of the pack, that ten of clubs will be one of them.

Lay out the cards on the floor so they're in the same design as the little pips on the face of the ten of clubs, like this –

When your partner comes back into the room, you point to any card and name it. Your partner says, 'No, that's not it.' You point to and name one or two other cards. Then you point to a certain spot on that ten of clubs. The spot you point to is the pip which has the same position on the ten of clubs as the card picked earlier has in the layout on the floor or table. (For example, if the chosen card is the one in the upper right-hand corner of the layout, then point to the pip in the upper right-hand corner as you touch the ten of clubs.) Your partner says 'No!'

Now you have secretly told your partner which card was chosen! You continue naming cards, and when you get around to pointing to that chosen one, your partner is able to say gleefully, '*That's* the card that was picked!'

Shape Up!

Here's what happens: your partner leaves the room.

You show six pieces of cardboard, each cut into a different shape. There is a circle, a cross, a triangle, a square, a star and a hexagon (which has six sides).

Someone picks up one of the shapes, shows it to everyone and then mixes it up with all the other shapes in a pile on the table.

Your partner is called back into the room. He or she picks up a pad and pencil, concentrates, and finally draws something on the pad.

You ask the person who picked the shape to find it and hold it up. Then your partner shows that the very same shape has been drawn on the pad!

Here's how you do it: use cardboard from the sides of cereal or soap-powder boxes and cut out the six shapes.

If you look at these six shapes, you'll see that each one has a numbered quality about it: the circle has ONE outside edge. The cross is made with TWO lines. The triangle has THREE sides. The square has FOUR sides. The star has FIVE points, and the hexagon has SIX sides. (You never call the audience's attention to these facts when you are performing, but you and your friend have memorized them.)

The two of you have also mentally divided the table top into six areas, as shown below.

Now you both know the secrets necessary to do the 'Shape Up!' trick.

Place the six shapes on the table top, but keep the pad in

your hands for the moment. Ask your partner to leave the room. Then ask someone to choose a shape and pick it up. Put that shape back with the others and mix 'em all in a pile.

As you call your partner back into the room, you *casually drop your pad on to the part of the table that signals the number of the chosen shape*. (In the picture, the person picked the cross, so the pad was placed in the number 2 spot.)

As soon as your friend picks up the pad, he or she knows (from where it was placed) which shape is the right one. But then your friend should pretend to think very hard before drawing that shape on the pad.

Number Mystery

Here's what happens: your friend leaves the room. Now you ask each of the other people to think of a number from 1 to 9. Whichever number is called out first will be the one you write on a small pad.

Tear off the sheet, crumple it up and drop it into a bowl. Ask everyone to remember that number.

Then you ask for more numbers, writing each one on a

sheet, crumpling it up and dropping it into the bowl, too. When you have six or seven, get someone to mix up the papers in the bowl.

Call your partner back into the room. He or she reaches into the bowl, concentrates, then removes one paper. Opening it, your partner asks who thought of the first number, and then shows that the one picked out of the bowl is the first number that was called.

Here's how you do it: when you begin the trick, you have a small bean hidden in your hand.

After you've written the first number, secretly sneak the bean inside the paper, crumple it up and drop it into the bowl.

Later, when reaching into the bowl to find the correct number, all your partner has to do is squeeze each paper until he or she finds the one with the hard bean in it, remove that one, open it (letting the bean slide secretly into the hand), and read off the number.

Mind-Reading Volunteer

Here's what happens: you have the group decide who should be the Mind-Reading Volunteer to help you with this test. You ask that person to come forward and sit with his or her back to the audience.

Now, three people in the audience each pick a card from a pack. They look at their cards and then put them back in the pack.

Handing the pack to the Volunteer, you say, 'Have you any idea which cards were picked?' Of course, the answer will be 'No'.

Then you ask the three people who chose cards to picture their cards in their minds as your Mind-Reading Volunteer tries to find them in the pack.

And finally, your wonderful Volunteer holds up three cards, and they are the ones that were chosen!

Your secret signal turned an ordinary member of the audience into a part of the act.

Here's how you do it: earlier in the day, write this message on a blank sticker (or on a tiny piece of paper) and glue it to the *face* of one of the Jokers in the pack –

Look through the pack and take out the 3 cards that are facing in the opposite direction from the others. Thank you for keeping this trick a secret!

Reverse this Joker (the one with the message on it) on the bottom of the pack so that it faces in towards the rest of the cards. Put the pack in its case, remembering which is the real top of the pack, and you're ready.

After your volunteer is seated with his or her back to the audience, have first one, then a second, then a third card taken from the pack. Make sure no one sees the reversed Joker on the bottom of the pack.

As you go back to the first person to have the card returned to the pack, *you secretly turn the pack over.* (Because the joker is face *in*, no one can tell that the pack is upside down.)

When the three cards are slid into the pack, *they'll be facing in the opposite direction from the rest of the cards.*

Take the pack to your mind-reader, and as you drop it into that person's lap, flip the top card (the Joker) over on top of the pack so that he or she can read the message.

The rest of the trick is up to your volunteer, and you will probably have a miracle!

DO YOU KNOW
THE SECRET?

These 'betchas' work because you are a step ahead of your friends. You alone know the sneaky way to meet the challenge. Practise each stunt at least once in private before you do it for real live people. Watch yourself in the mirror. Then you'll not only know the secret, but you'll be able to make it work for you!

Switch!

Ask your friend to hold his or her arms out sideways, parallel to the floor, and to make them stiff. Put a book in one of your friend's hands and say, 'I'll betcha can't transfer that book to

45

the other hand without bending your arms either at the elbow or at the shoulder.' Most likely, your friend won't be able to do it. But you will!

Here's the secret: hold your arms out in that same position, with the book in one hand. Switch the book to the other hand by bending your knees, tilting your body, and plopping the book down on a table. Then turn your body so that your other arm is facing the table. Once again, bend your knees and tilt your body (keep those arms stiff). Then pick up the book in your other hand!

Four from Four

Here's a tricky trick. Can you take 4 away from 4, and still be left with 8?

The secret: take a square piece of paper, and tear off the four corners – you will end up with eight corners! If we were to tear off the original four corners in the picture (A, B, C and D), we'd be left with eight new ones!

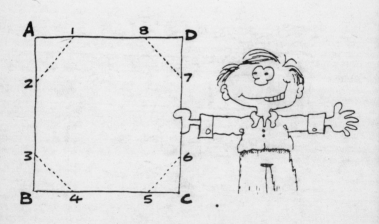

Strong Finger, Weak Fists

Say to your friend, 'Put one fist on top of the other.' When he or she has done that, say, 'I'll betcha I can knock your fists apart with one finger.' Then, with your index finger, stroke (gently hit) your friend's top fist right off the bottom one!

Now you say, 'I'll betcha can't do that to me.' You put one fist on top of the other, and your friend can't knock them apart!

Here's the secret: when you put one fist on top of the other, stick the thumb of your bottom hand up into the top fist and grip it tightly for support. (Don't let anyone see you doing this!) Strike as he or she will, your friend won't be able to separate your fists.

47

CRAZY COINS

A trickster who knows a couple of stunts that can be done with coins is always ready for action. You can reach into your pocket any time, anywhere, and pull out your props. Two of these crazy coin betchas are line-'em-ups, two are puzzling coin games (that you can always win), and the last, Catchy Coins, is a juggling stunt.

Line-'em-ups

Place twelve coins in a square so that there are four coins in each row. Now, can you move these coins into another figure that has *five* coins in each row?

Lay six coins so that they are touching one another in two rows, three on top, three on the bottom, as in the picture.

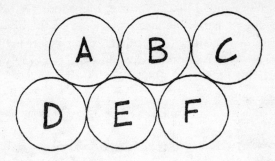

Can you change these two rows of coins into a circle of six coins in only three moves? The rules are: handle only one coin at a time without moving any other. When a coin is moved, it must still touch two other coins in its new position.

The secret: first move coin A so that it's above (and touching) coins B and C. Next, move B so that it rests above D and E. Last, shift coin D so that it is in between A and B.

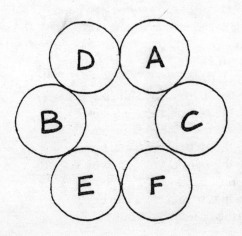

Coin Games

This is a puzzle if you don't know how, a game if you do.

Start by drawing a long rectangle. Make four vertical lines (up and down) across the inside of the rectangle, dividing it into five boxes, one next to the other. Put a 1p piece in the first box, and one in the second. Leave the third box empty. Put a 2p piece in the fourth and fifth boxes.

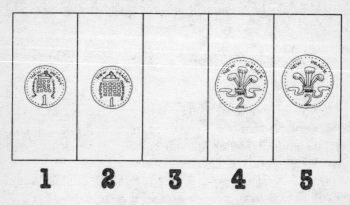

The object is to move the 1p pieces into the 2p boxes, and the 2p pieces into the 1p boxes – in only eight moves. Either a slide of a coin from one box to another or a jump over another coin (as in draughts) is considered one move.

Try it, and then (and only then) do I give you permission to read the solution.

The secret moves:

(1) Slide the 1p from box 2 into box 3.
(2) Jump the 2p from box 4 into box 2.
(3) Slide the 2p from box 5 into box 4.
(4) Jump the 1p from box 3 into box 5.
(5) Jump the 1p from box 1 into box 3.
(6) Slide the 2p from box 2 into box 1.
(7) Jump the 2p from box 4 into box 2.
(8) Slide the 1p from box 3 into box 4.

Heads and Tails

Place six coins on a table so that the first three are heads up, the next three, tails up. Can you turn the coins over – *two at a time* and touching only coins that are neighbours – so that they wind up alternating heads-tails-heads-tails-heads-tails?

Here's the secret: first turn over coins 3 and 4. Then turn over coins 4 and 5. Now turn over coins 2 and 3. Congratulations! You now have your coins heads-tails-heads-tails-heads-tails.

Catchy Coins

This juggling stunt will really impress your friends, and it's so simple that you should be able to do it by the third try.

Holding your hand palm up, place a little pile of coins on your elbow. Cup your hand, so it forms a little pocket aimed at

your elbow. Now drop your elbow (suddenly and with a smooth circular swing of your arm). This will bring your hand to just below where your elbow was, and you'll catch the pile of coins.

It won't work the first time, but, by the second or third, you'll find that you'll be able to catch the coins neatly and cleanly.

The real secret is not to throw the coins either up or out, but just to *sweep the hand down and drop the elbow* quickly out from under the coins. *Your hand will simply be where the coins are.* If you haven't got it by the second try, bend your knees a little as you do the stunt.

Keep track of how many coins you end up catching. Perhaps you can even break the world record!

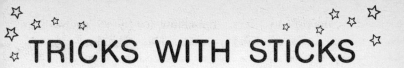

TRICKS WITH STICKS

All these stunts can be done with toothpicks, cotton buds, paper clips, blades of grass, or whatever sticks you have to hand.

This pattern of thirteen squares is made with thirty-six sticks. Can you remove just eight sticks so that you wind up with a pattern of six squares instead of the original thirteen?

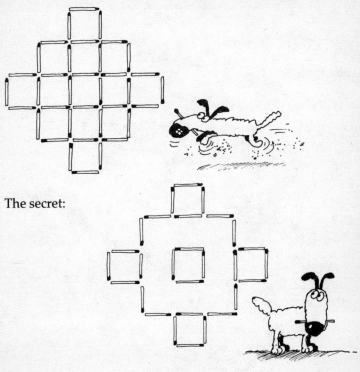

The secret:

Place twenty-four sticks so that they form nine squares. Can you take away eight sticks, leaving only two squares?

The secret:

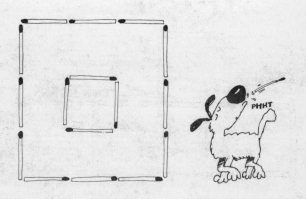

With twelve sticks, form four squares. Can you rearrange them to make three squares by moving only three sticks? (Don't remove any sticks.)

The secret:

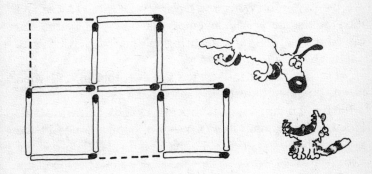

Water, Water Everywhere

Water, water everywhere but not a drop to drink – unless your friends figure out how to do this stunt.

Put a glass full of water on a table, cover it with a saucer, and then top the saucer with an empty glass. Say, 'I'll betcha you can't drink that glass of water using only one hand, which may not touch the saucer.'

Let each of your friends try to solve this problem, and when no one can, then show them the solution.

Put two flat-topped chairs back to back and a little way apart. Pick up the bottom glass (which will automatically lift the saucer and the top glass). Slip this bottom glass between the two chair backs. This will slide the saucer along the top of the two chairs so that it rests on the backs, supporting the top glass. Now you can remove the bottom glass and drink it to the last drop.

GROANERS

Some stunts make folks grin. Others make 'em groan. Do you like groaners? Those are the dumb gags and sucker bets that have jerky, jokey solutions (like the one where you say to a friend, 'I'll bet you 20p you can't take off your coat alone.' And then, as soon as your friend starts taking off his or her coat, you just take off your coat, too).

Friends always groan when you tell them groaners – and then they turn round and pull the same gag on the very next person they meet! Here are a dozen dopey dares.

(1) Say to a friend: 'I'll betcha I can stay under water for a full minute.' And when your friend forks out a coin to cover the bet, you simply fill a glass with water and place it over your head.

(2) Challenge someone: 'I'll betcha you can't say fish with your mouth closed.' And when they are all done doing rotten imitations of a ventriloquist, you simply say, 'Fish with your mouth closed.'

(3) You can bet anybody this: 'I can stick out my tongue and touch my ear.' And then all you do is stick out your tongue, and (with your hand) touch your ear.

(4) Or you can boast: 'I'll betcha I can jump across the street' – and then what you do is go across the street and then jump a couple of times.

(5) You say to your friend: 'Give me a 1p piece, and without looking at it, I'll be able to tell you the date.' And unless your friend has heard this trick before, he or she will give you a coin and will expect to be told the date on it. But what you'll do is tell your friend the date of *that day*. After all, you never said you were going to tell your friend the date on the 1p piece, did you?

(6) Get a friend into the kitchen. On the table have butter, eggs, and all the other things that a person needs to make an omelette, together with a frying pan. (I'm just assuming your kitchen has a stove as well.)

Say, 'I'll betcha that you can't make an omelette with these ingredients. In fact, I'll betcha the best cook in the world will not be able to make an omelette with them.' Your friend will discover you're right when he or she breaks open the eggs and finds that you have already boiled them, so that they are very hard!

(7) Bet somebody ten pounds that he or she can't answer 'a hard-boiled egg' to three questions that you'll ask. First ask any two silly questions that you can think of. Your third question should be, 'Which would you rather win, this ten-pound bet or a hard-boiled egg?' If your friend says, 'A hard-boiled egg,' hand over the hard-boiled egg. If your friend says, 'The ten pounds,' he or she loses the bet and the money!

(8) Can you read minds? No? I can't either, but when I was a kid I used to pretend I could.

I'd say to a friend, 'I'm going to read your mind.' And then I'd make a motion on a pad of paper as though I were writing what the other person was thinking. What I was actually writing on the paper was the word 'No', but as I wrote it, I'd move my hand around the paper so my friend couldn't tell what I was scribbling.

Then I'd say, 'Do you know what I wrote on this piece of paper?' The other person would, of course, say 'No', and then I'd triumphantly say, 'I read your mind – I knew you were going to say that! See?' And I'd turn my pad around and show my friend that 'No' was exactly what I had written on the piece of paper.

(9) You can make this claim: 'I will make you clasp your hands together in such a way that it will be impossible for you to leave the room without *unclasping* your hands.' Here's how you can do it: clasp your friend's hands around a pole, a piano leg, or anything immovable.

(10) Tell the group that your pencil has a special magic point. If someone will name a colour, your pencil will write that colour. Let us say that a person names 'red'. What you do is write the *word* 'red' on the piece of paper, and indeed, your pencil *did* write that colour!

Make sure that when you finish this trick you take a very deep bow. That's the only way you'll avoid being hit by the things your friends will throw at you.

(11) Say to a friend: 'I'll betcha I have a piece of paper with some handwriting on it for which you would quickly pay four

pounds.' And when your friend argues, simply pull out a five-pound note and point to the signature of the Chief Cashier of the Bank of England.

(12) Then say: 'I'll betcha I can stand on the same piece of newspaper that you're standing on, and you won't be able to touch me, even though I'm only a few inches away.' When your friend gives up, spread a sheet of newspaper over the door sill, close the door nearly all the way, and you and your friend will be in different rooms. You can stand on the same paper, but he or she will not be able to touch you through the almost closed door.

BETCHA CAN'T
TRICKS

There is an old familiar song (well, *I'm* familiar with it) that goes 'Nothing is impossible, not if you dream, etc., etc., etc.' Well, in my opinion, all the etc.'s may be true but the lyrics are not.

Lots of things are impossible.
– It's impossible to travel faster than the speed of light.
– It's impossible for a person to stay awake indefinitely.
– It's impossible to put your elbow in your mouth.
– It's impossible to put an egg together after you crack the shell.
– And have you ever tried putting toothpaste back into a tube?

Here are some challenges. Unless you are double-jointed, there's no way that you can do these stunts. But they're fun to pull on your friends, because they all sound so simple, and only you know they are impossible.

Off the Top of Your Head

A seven-stone weakling (like, say, me) can place her index finger on top of her head, and a big guy, pulling on her wrist with all his strength, using one hand, will not be able to lift that finger off her head.

There are only two rules: he must not jerk the wrist (he is allowed only to pull with a steady tug), and he can't brace his elbows against his body.

No Jerks!

Touch the tips of your two index fingers together in front of you, with your elbows out. Your friend will find that – holding your wrists and pulling without jerking – he or she cannot separate your fingers.

The Weak Spot

Ask your friend to stand up. Say, 'I'm going to put my index finger at a point on your face, and I promise that you will not be able to move forward. The only rule is this: you may not move your feet.'

And you can keep your promise. Here's the secret: *place your index finger sideways under your friend's nose* and keep your arm straight and stiff. It's a very delicate spot and, unless your friend is a great deal stronger than you are, you'll win the bet.

Touch the Tips

Close your eyes. Stretch your arms out to the sides. Point your index fingers in towards the centre. Bend your elbows and bring your fingertips together without opening your eyes. Oddly enough, it's almost impossible. It's not *impossibly* impossible. I mean, I did it a couple of times. But, whether you bring your fingers together slowly or quickly, it's really hard to make the tips of those fingers touch. Your friends won't believe that this is hard until they try.

Jack Can't Jump over the Candlestick

Here's a simple-sounding but sly challenge that just can't be met.

You hold up a small object (a coin, pencil, wallet, or whatever) and say, 'I'll betcha I can put this thing on the floor in such a way that no one – absolutely no one – can jump over it. Is it a bet?' And when your friend agrees, you just put the article on the floor, *touching the wall*.

Meet You Half-way

When I'm writing stunts for a book or a newspaper column, I scribble my notes on a yellow pad and then dictate the stuff I've scribbled into a tiny dictating machine. The fun for me is watching people's faces as they hear me dictate these stunts. Invariably, their eyes start to shift, looking for whatever prop I'm talking about; or their fingers rise as they unconsciously think through the stunt, doubting that I could possibly be right.

Now this next stunt is unbelievable. And as I dictated it, I saw my daughter rise, leave the room, and come back with a ruler. She just had to try it. It worked. It'll work for you, too.

Here's what you say: 'Put your index fingers under the far ends of a one-foot ruler and close your eyes. Now (with your eyes still closed) bring your fingers together. They will meet right at the six-inch mark.' As a matter of fact, it's impossible for anyone to make them meet at any other point. And when the metric system really comes into full swing, and your ruler no longer reads 'one-foot', your fingers will still meet smack in the middle of the stick.

The Mighty Toothpick

Say to someone, 'Think you're strong, eh? I'll bet you can't even break a wooden toothpick.'

Then put a wooden toothpick under your friend's index finger, over the middle finger, and under the ring finger. Tell the person to keep the thumb out to the side.

In this position, it's really impossible to break that skinny little wooden toothpick (at least, I haven't met anyone who can do it). Are you a member of some splinter group that can?

Knuckle Under (1)

Put the fingertips of your right hand so that they are touching the fingertips of your left hand. Bend in half your middle fingers (the ones between your index and ring fingers on each hand) and place them so that both middle-finger knuckles are touching (see the picture).

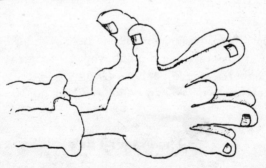

You must keep these knuckles together.

You'll find that you can separate your thumbs without pulling the knuckles apart – and that you can separate your index fingers and your little fingers, but it is impossible (if you keep your knuckles touching) to separate your ring fingers.

I just lied. I can do it. So can you if you're double-jointed. But if you and your friends are normal, regular people without funny fingers, you'll find that you absolutely cannot separate those ring fingers without pulling your middle-finger knuckles apart.

Knuckle Under (2)

Have your friend place his or her hand so that the fingertips are on the table with the middle finger tucked under (see picture).

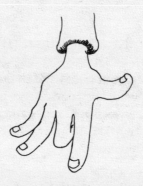

Then say, 'You can lift your little finger without lifting the others, you can raise your thumb, you can wiggle your index finger, but your ring finger is very heavy, isn't it? Try to lift it. Doesn't it feel as if it weighs pounds and pounds?'

The Finger Trick

Think you're mixed up now? Wait until you try this stunt. Hold your arms down in front of you. Cross the wrists and clasp all your fingers together. Bring your hands in towards your body and keep bringing them up (bending your elbows), until your fingers are on the top.

Here's the mixed-up part of this stunt. You'll now find that your fingers are so confused about where they are that they won't be able to move. Don't believe me, eh? OK – ask someone to point to any one of your fingers without actually touching it. Now you try to move that finger. No luck, right?

This is all the more amazing when you consider that you've had that finger with you all your life!

Betchas With Notes

Here are some 'impossibles' to do with five-pound notes that can't fail to keep your friends amused. If you haven't got a five-pound note of your own, persuade your Mum or Dad to lend you one. Tell them not to worry: the tricks are so reliable that you can guarantee the fiver will be returned safely!

Catch-a-Note

It is impossible to catch a falling five-pound note if you do the following: crease the five-pound note vertically (up and down) and grasp it at the top with your thumb and index finger. Now ask your friend to place one hand behind his or her back and hold the other hand so that the palm is open and next to the note but not touching it. You drop the note. Your friend will not be able to catch it because, in the split second it takes to react, the note will already have slipped past the palm.

A Powerful Piece of Paper

You say, 'I'll betcha you can't fix a five-pound note so that it will be absolutely impossible to tear.' And when your friends finish trying, here's what you do: start rolling the note from one of the corners, until the note is tightly wound up. When it's all in a compact roll, it is absolutely impossible to tear! (Well, Superman could tear it, but I can't, and I'll bet you can't either.)

So Near and Yet So Far

Ask a friend to stand with heels against the wall and knees straight. Drop a five-pound note (or a ten-pound note, if you wish – you're safe!) right in front of the person. Now say, 'If you can pick up that note without bending your knees – just bend over, pick it up, and stand up again – you can keep it.'

Don't sweat – the money is yours.

The Blow Hard Card

Since most magicians do tricks with playing cards, I thought you'd like to learn a trick that you can't do with a playing card.

Start with a card from an incomplete pack. (Oh please, I beg of you, don't be a joker and use a card from one of your parents' good packs or they'll never forgive me!)

Bend the card down about ¾ inch in from the edge of both sides. Stand it up on those two small ends, as you see in the picture.

Now, here's the trick that can't be done. You can challenge your friends to blow as hard as they wish, but, no matter how much they blow, the card will remain standing on its own two little legs! It can't be blown over.

A Note in a Book

Since I started writing about betchas and challenges, and doing them on TV chat shows, people constantly stop me in the street and say, 'Here's how I used to do it.' And 'it' is usually a stunt similar to one I've recently done.

The latest 'here's-how-I-used-to-do-it' I was shown looks so-o-o easy – and it's really so-o-o hard. I think it's actually a 'how-I-used-to-try-to-do-it', because I haven't seen anyone succeed in doing this stunt.

You put a five-pound note into a book and balance the book on end. With your hands behind your back, you stand on one foot and lean forward. The object is to try to pick the five-pound note out of the book with your teeth.

If you can get it, you can keep it – but until you actually *do* get it, don't bank on it.

FOR YOUR
EYES ONLY

In the language of spies, a 'cleartext' is any message that is meant to be read exactly as it is written. For example, this sentence is in cleartext.

However, there are some great ways to write a note in cleartext so that it can only be read by the person who is supposed to read it, because only that person is in on a special secret.

Shuffled Message

Here is one of the cleverest ways that you can imagine to hide a message!

Shuffle an old discarded pack of cards and then make a list of the cards from the top to the bottom. You can do it much faster if you use abbreviations – like A for ace, K for king, C for clubs, H for hearts, S for spades, D for diamonds, and so on. Your list should look something like this: AC, 2S, 5H, 7C, 10D, 4H, 8C, 9C, 2D, AH . . .

Give a copy of the list to each friend with whom you may want to exchange secret messages.

To write a message, arrange an old pack of cards so that it is in the same order as your list. With a *pencil*, write your message on the side edges of the pack, writing two lines on each of the four sides, if you have to.

Also, mark a straight line in one corner so that the line goes across the corners of all the cards. Shuffle the pack three or four times and hand it or send it to your friend.

When your friend is alone, he or she arranges the pack so that it once again matches the list, and then the message can be read. If the words aren't clear, your friend should look for the line on the marked corner and make sure that all the cards are turned in the right direction.

Secret on a Stick

The commanders of the Roman and Greek armies generally carried a metal rod decorated with fancy ends. This 12- to 14-inch-long stick was called a *scytale*. Only very important generals were allowed to carry these batons.

When one of these military men had to send a secret message to his brother officer, he would wrap a strip of paper around the scytale and then write whatever he had to say *down the length of the rod*. When the paper was unwound, it looked like gibberish instead of an important message. But when the other officer got this silly-looking strip of paper, he'd wrap it around the rod, and read the private message.

You can do the same thing and send notes across a room – notes that can't be read by anyone who gets hold of them along the way. Here's how.

Get two matching unsharpened pencils (that way they're sure to be the same length). Give one to your friend and keep the other for yourself.

To send your message, cut a 1-inch strip from the long side of a sheet of typing paper.

Wrap the paper diagonally around the pencil as tightly as possible, leaving less than ¼ inch between each edge on every twist.

Fasten the end of the wrapped paper with the tiniest possible bit of sellotape.

Now write the message in a straight line along the side of the pencil, putting only one letter between every two edges, and some letters right on the edges.

The message can be two or three lines long, depending on the thickness of the pencil.

Now remove the tape and unwrap the paper. All that anyone can see is a mixture of letters and squiggles scattered along the edges of the strip of paper. Half a letter will show up in one place, half in another.

When your friend gets the message, he or she can read it by wrapping the paper around a pencil like this: hold the strip so that the letters are upright. Start rolling at the bottom and twist as tightly as possible around the pencil. Don't try to read or make sense of the message as it is rolled – just match up the random lines so that they form letters, and fit the letters together so that they make words. Then place a tiny piece of tape at the end of the strip, and the secret message will be there for you to see.

If you would like to send a *long* secret message (for example, as a letter) you and your friend will need matching pieces of dowel, or broomsticks.

Instead of tiny strips of paper, try to get hold of some adding machine paper. Then in the same way you can send your Secret On A Stick!

Skip-a-Letter

Here's a very easy way to disguise a message. It's easy to read when you know the rule, but it's confusing to the 'enemy'.

On a sheet of paper, write down your message. Count the letters. Divide the total number by 2. Got the sum? That's the middle of your message. Go back to the beginning and count off that number of letters, then draw a line between that and the next letter. (In other words, if your message is 22 letters long, you would draw a line between the 11th and 12th letters.)

On another sheet of paper, write your message in capital letters, *leaving enough space between each letter for another letter*.

When you get to the line marking the centre of the message, *go back to the beginning of your message and start putting in the rest of the letters between the ones you've already written.*

Your friend can read the message by writing down the odd letters (letters 1, 3, 5, etc.) from the beginning to the end. Then your friend goes back to the beginning to write down the even letters, which make up the *second* half of the message.

TIHTITSEMNECSOSRARGEECITSLWYR

If you think someone may be catching on to the method, write the message backwards!

!TSIDRRWASWIKECNAOBSNIEHTT

Now You See It, Now You Don't: Invisible Writing

For hundreds of years, spies have sent messages written in invisible ink.

The most common ingredient for invisible ink is the juice of any of the citrus fruits (lemon, orange, grapefruit, lime). If you have one of these fruits in your house you can create a message that's here today and gone tomorrow!

You will need: citrus fruit juice (squeezed into a teaspoon), a wooden toothpick and a sheet of paper.

Dip the end of the toothpick into the juice and gently write the first letter of your message on the paper. Make sure you write without pressing down so you don't leave scratches on the paper. Dip the toothpick again and write the second letter. You'll need to dip your 'pen' into the juice for each letter, so that it will show clearly when it is 'developed' later.

Then let the juice dry completely. To develop one of these invisible messages, all you have to do is expose the paper to heat. Holding it over a large light bulb will usually make the writing appear. Another way is to have an adult iron the paper with the iron at a medium setting.

A good way to disguise the message is to write a regular letter in between the lines of your invisible message.

Wet 'n' Wild

Here is an invisible writing method that doesn't use *any* ink.

Dip the paper you want to use for your message in warm water. Lay the wet paper on a smooth surface (like a kitchen worktop or bathroom counter or glass table top). Place a dry sheet of paper over the wet one.

With a ballpoint pen write your message.

Remove the dry top sheet of paper and throw it away. Let your wet bottom sheet dry out. The secret message will be invisible, but take my word for it – it will be there!

To 'develop' one of these Wet 'n' Wild message sheets, just dip the paper into water again. Now hold it up to a light. You will see the message you wrote, but it will be in lines of light. This is a watermark, and it's done in the same way that paper-makers mark their stationery so that people will recognize their product.

By the way, when the paper dries, the message will once again disappear!

Reflect on This

This method for hiding a message works like magic.

Clean a little mirror (one in a compact is a good size) until it is beautifully clear.

Sharpen a piece of soap so it has a point like a pencil, then write a short message on the mirror. Make your letters a little larger than usual because they'll smear a bit.

Now rub the writing with a cotton wool ball until the letters disappear. *But as soon as the letters are gone, stop rubbing!*

Now the compact or mirror will look clean and will pass any kind of inspection. Keep it in your purse or pocket until you hand it to someone.

To develop the message, all your friend has to do is *breathe on the mirror*. What's left of the letters will stand out for reading, and afterwards he or she can clean off the evidence.

Do you think anyone will see through that?

Camouflaged Cartoons

The top-secret sketches on the next page are catchy clues. Each one represents some kind of a picture, but not what you might think. When you've worked out what they are, draw them for your friends and see if they can guess them!

ANSWER: (reading from left to right, top row to bottom row): A bubble-gum champ, germs avoiding a friend who caught an antibody, a very close photograph of a camel passing a pyramid, a person playing a trombone in a telephone booth, noughts and crosses played by one person, two times four.

Here are two letters your spies have intercepted. Can you read them?

ANSWERS:
Dear Aunt Belle:
   Can you be here for tea before Jean's train leaves?

   Yes, I can.

Hidden Meanings, Hidden Sayings

The shapes of the words or the positions of words in relation to
one another are clues to the answers.

For example:
    R
R O A D ANSWER: Crossroads
    A
    D

STAND **I**	**GROUND** **FEET** **FEET** **FEET** **FEET** **FEET** **FEET** **FEET**	**MAN** **BOARD**
DICE **DICE**		**ESGGESGG**
		MEAL 1 MEAL 1

BUSINESS PLEASURE

CYCLE
CYCLE
CYCLE

ANSWERS: (reading top to bottom down the columns): I
understand, a pair of dice, the worm turns, six feet under-
ground, business before pleasure, man overboard, two
scrambled eggs, one after every meal, tricycle.

Secret Sillies

Can you decipher these two coded messages?

YYUR
YYUB
ICUR
YY 4 Me

IO04I80

ANSWERS:

> Too wise you are,
> Too wise you be,
> I see you are,
> Too wise for me.

> I owe nothing for I ate nothing.

Computer Punchlines

Way back in the fifteenth century, a genius named Leonardo da Vinci studied everything around him. Once he had found out how something worked, he then tried to invent a way to make it better. During his studies he filled many notebooks, but for hundreds of years no one could read them. Why? Because he had simply written them backwards. That's usually called 'mirror writing'. You have to hold the writing in front of a mirror in order to read it.

Today you can do almost the same thing by using your electronic calculator. Certain numbers look like letters when they are upside down. Here are those numbers and the letters they resemble:

1 I
3 E
4 h
5 S
7 L
8 B
0 O

See if you can make the stories on the following pages add up to the proper words.

(1) A man went fishing and had a very good day. He caught 15 trout, 150 bass, 95 halibut, 55 perch, and 2 old tyres. Actually, his story was a –.

$15 + 150 + 95 + 55 + 2 =$

(2) A man told his workers to pick the 1,377 trees in each of his 4 orchards by the end of the week. They did it because he was the –.

$1,377 \times 4 =$

(3) What is it that has 4 wings, flies 13 miles per hour, travels about 300 miles per day, has 6 legs, 3 eyes, and about 12 stripes?

$4 + 13 + 300 + 6 + 3 + 12 =$

(4) Five men took turns steering a boat for 101 miles each. At the end of that time a storm came up and they had to send out an –.

$5 \times 101 =$

(5) A farmer bought 10 acres of land at £710.50 each, because he liked the –.

$10 \times 710.50 =$

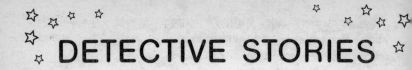

Here are some detective stories for you to tell your friends. But first you have to solve them. So get your thinking cap and your detective's raincoat and read on.

The Escape

Two friends are in the same jail cell. They're desperately looking for a way to escape. Their cell has no windows – just a skylight with no bars. They know that if they can get to the skylight, they can escape through it. Unfortunately, it's so high that even when they stand on each other's shoulders on the bed (which is the only piece of furniture in the room) they can't reach the skylight. So they take one of the bed legs and start to dig a tunnel. Soon they realize that they'll have to dig too far to escape.

Just as they're about to give up, one of them shouts, 'I have it!'

What was his idea? What did they do? How did they escape? You now have all the clues.

Solution: they dug a tunnel in order to gather lots of earth above the ground. And then they piled the earth up, climbed on top of that mountain of earth, reached the skylight, and escaped!

What Happened Here?

When you try this mystery on your friends, you can only say 'yes' or 'no' in answer to their questions. No explanations!

Say to your friends, 'The mystery is this: Jack walks into the house, heads for the sitting-room, opens the door, and here is what he sees: the window is open. Water and broken glass are on the floor. Sam and Mary are lying there, dead. What happened?'

No! Don't read on – try to work it out.

Give up?

Solution: something has knocked the fish tank off the table on to the floor, breaking it and spilling the water. Sam and Mary? They are goldfish.

Slow Boat

A man wished to buy the slowest boat made in the United States. He placed an advertisement to that effect in the local paper. Three captains answered his ad. To decide which boat was the slowest, he told the three captains to race across the lake and back. The three set out. By the end of the day, none of them had come back. Each was trying to prove that his boat was the slowest.

How should the man have arranged the race to find out which boat really was the slowest?

Solution: the man should have asked each captain to pilot *another* boat, not his own. Then each captain would have been sure to go as fast as possible in this other boat in order to prove that his own boat was the slowest.

'Don't Shoot Me, John'

Several shots are heard just after a voice says pleadingly, 'Don't shoot me, John.' When the police get into the room, they find a lawyer, a doctor, an army lieutenant and a milkman. A gun is on the floor. The police immediately arrest the milkman. What could there be about the lawyer, doctor and lieutenant that makes the police so sure that the milkman was the one who fired the gun?

Solution: the lawyer, doctor and army lieutenant are women. The only person who could logically have been called John is the milkman.

Clean and Dirty

Two miners came out of a coal shaft. One came out dirty; the other was clean. The one who was clean went over to a pump and washed himself. Strangely enough, the one who was dirty went home without washing. How can you account for this?

Solution: the dirty miner looked at the clean miner, assumed he was clean too, and didn't think it was necessary for him to wash himself.

The Bus Driver

You're driving a bus, and 32 people get on. Then 14 people get off. After that, 130 people get on. Next, 9 people get off. Then 2 people get on and 120 people get off. At the next stop 19 people get on. Finally, 36 people get off.

The question is this: what colour are the bus driver's eyes?

Solution: the bus driver's eyes are whatever colour your eyes are. After all, the first thing I said was, 'You're driving a bus!'

The Grateful Cowboy

This mystery isn't really a hard nut to crack. It's a scene from an old Western film. A cowboy walks into a bar. The bartender pulls out a gun, and the cowboy says, 'Thank you!' Why?

Solution: the man who walked into the bar had hiccups, and the bartender pulled the gun to scare the cowboy out of his hiccups.

Double Trouble

Two boys fill out registration forms for summer camp. The registrar sees that they have the same parents, live at the same address and have the same date of birth. The only difference is that one is named Tony and the other is Adam. When asked, 'Are you twins?' they both say, 'No.' If their answers are accurate and they both have the same mother and father, how can they not be twins?

Solution: Tony and Adam are two of a set of triplets.

The Lift Enigma

A man gets into a lift on the seventh floor and pushes a button. He goes down to the ground floor, gets out, and goes to work. At the end of the day, when he comes home, he gets into the same lift, pushes a button, goes to the fifth floor and walks up two more floors. Why?

Solution: the man is a midget. He could reach the low button for the ground floor, but he lives on the seventh and can't reach up to the button for his own floor.

The Dry Diamond

Mrs Honeyfinger was working in the kitchen when her diamond ring slipped off her finger and fell smack into some coffee. Strange to say, the diamond did not get wet. Why not?

Solution: the ring fell into a jar of dry ground coffee.

The Cinema Surprise

Mrs Lindo left the cinema and walked towards the unlit car park where she had left her car. There were no artificial lights or moonlight, yet she was able to spot her car about seventy-five yards away. How was she able to see it?

Solution: she had been to an afternoon performance and it was broad daylight.

RIDDLERS

Riddles were popular even thousands of years ago, in the days of Aesop. Of course, in those days they weren't used for fun, but rather to decide which country would be able to tax the other and who would be king.

When Aesop was working for the ruler Lycurgus, the king of Egypt once sent this riddle to Lycurgus: 'If you can send someone to build a tower high into the air – one that touches neither earth nor heaven – then you can collect three years' taxes from me. If you cannot, I will collect ten years' tribute from you.'

Aesop said to Lycurgus, 'Answer him: "I will send you men to build your tower when the winter is over."'

Then Aesop gave orders for four young eagles to be taught to carry boys on their backs. When fully grown, they would fly into the air, carrying the boys, with cords attached to them so they were under the control of the boys and would go wherever the boys wished.

Summer came, and Aesop, boys and eagles (together with lots of servants and equipment intended to impress the Egyptians) left for Egypt. They said to the king of Egypt, 'We're ready to build your tower. Point out the place.' The bewildered king pointed to a field and gave measurements for the building. Aesop put one eagle at each corner of the field. The boys mounted and the eagles flew up into the air. When the boys were aloft, Aesop said to the king, 'Now, if you can work out how to give them the mud, bricks, wood, and whatever else is required for the building, they are in position to start building a tower that will touch neither earth nor sky.'

Of course the king could not get the materials up to the boys and eagles who were waiting, so he lost the bet.

The Riddlers you'll find here aren't matters of life and death. Your friends will have fun racking their brains trying to guess the answer, and you'll feel rather clever, since you were the one who asked the Riddler.

(1) You have a ball. You throw it away from you as hard as you can. It doesn't hit anything, nor does anybody catch it, but it comes back to you. There are no strings or elastic involved. Why does the ball come back?

Answer: because you threw it up instead of forward or backward.

(2) A man built a house with four sides. Each side had a southern exposure. A big bear approached the house. What colour was the bear, and how do you know?

Answer: the bear was a white polar bear. We know that because the house had four southern exposures. That means the house had to be built at the North Pole.

(3) A man went to see a film. He found the film so boring that he fell asleep. He dreamed that a lion was chasing him. He had a heart attack and died in his sleep. What's wrong with this story?

Answer: if the man died, how could anyone have known what he was dreaming?

(4) What is it from which you may take away the whole and still have some left, or take away some and have the whole left?

Answer: the word 'wholesome'.

(5) What is neither inside the house nor outside the house, and yet the house wouldn't be complete without it?

Answer: windows.

(6) How can you show someone what he or she never saw, what you never saw, what nobody ever saw, and which after you have both seen it, nobody else will see again?

Answer: get a nut, crack open the shell, and take out the kernel (neither of you ever saw it before, nor did anyone else). Pop the kernel into your mouth and eat it (nobody will ever see it again).

(7) The father is four times as old as his son. Twenty years from now, the father will be twice as old as his son. How old are the father and the son today?

Answer: the father is forty; the son is ten. In twenty years, the father will be sixty, while the son will be thirty.

(8) Lying there in the yard so neat
   Was something very good to eat.
   It had neither flesh nor bone
   But in twenty-one days, it walked alone.

What is it?

Answer: an egg.

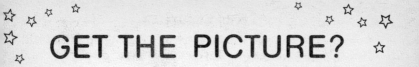

GET THE PICTURE?

People confidently say, 'When I see it, I'll believe it,' but that's not necessarily so. You can't always believe your eyes because your eyes can be tricked – by shapes, by shadows, and even by suggestions from the mind, which often insists on seeing what it *thinks* it should be seeing.

Here are some stunts that will make your friends say, 'I can't believe my eyes!'

Up a Tree

What is this?

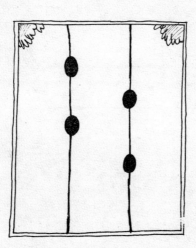

Answer: a bear climbing a tree. (Get it? The bear's round the other side and all we can see are the four paws.)

Try to Picture This

Just think about this one: if you take a rectangle of paper and fold it in half and then again in the same direction and then a third time, how many creases will be on that piece of paper when you open it up?

Answer: seven creases.

The Missing Arrow

Adding only two straight lines, can you make a third arrow just like the two in the picture?

Answer:

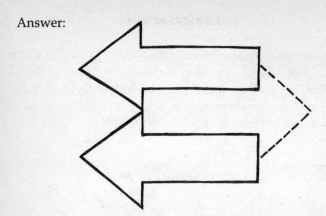

Penny for Your Thoughts

Say to a friend: 'Do you have a 1p piece? Look at it. Now look at the table top in this picture. It looks bigger than a 1p piece, doesn't it? Want to bet? I'll betcha there's no way that you can put your coin down on the table in this picture without its sides touching the edges of the table top.' (There's no trick to this – it can't be done. The size of the table top is an optical illusion.)

Baffling Boxes

Can you cross off six lines to make ten?

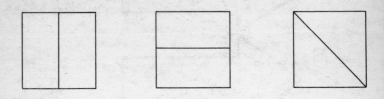

Here's how it can be done:

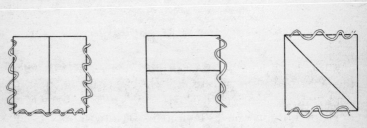

Now you can draw squares like this and stump your friends.

1000 the Hard Way

Betcha can't write 1000 in numbers without lifting your pencil from the paper.

Give up? Here's how it's done: fold down a flap at the top of a sheet of paper. Draw the '1' of the 1000 so that it extends past the edge. Without lifting your pencil, continue the line up on to the flap for a loop. That will become the first '0'. Do the same for the next two '0's.

Now lift the flap and you have drawn your 1000 without lifting your pencil from the paper.

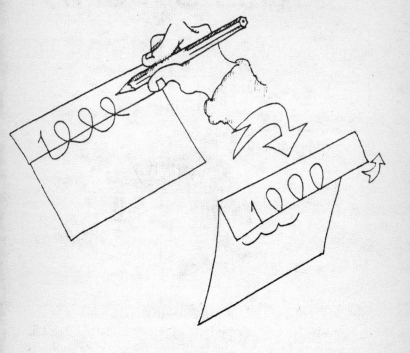

SECRET LINGOES

Pig Latin

Pig Latin is probably the most common artificial language used in English. No one is sure how or where it started, but kids have been talking back and forth with these funny-sounding words for generations.

It's a simple language and uses just three rules.

(1) When a word begins with a consonant, put the consonant at the end of the word, and add the sound of 'ay', like in the word 'play'. For example, book = ook-bay; table = able-tay; me = ee-may.

(2) If a word begins with two consonants that make a single sound ('th', 'sh', etc.), move them both to the end, and then add the 'ay' sound. For example, that = at-thay; should = ood-shay; speak = eak-spay. This is used for all words beginning with bl, br, ch, cl, cr, fl, fr, and so on.

(3) If the word begins with a vowel, instead of adding the

'ay' sound, you use 'way'. For example, I = eye-way; on = on-way; are = are-way.

Ow-hay ast-fay an-cay ou-yay eak-spay ig-pay atin-lay?

As-way ast-fay as-way ou-yay an-cay!

Local Lingoes

There are several tongue-twisting languages that are spoken by American kids only in certain areas, like on the East Coast or in the deep South. Almost all these lingoes work by doing something funny with the first vowel found in each word.

'TURKEY IRISH' is spoken by using the following rule: add the sound of 'ab' (like in 'jab') *before* the first vowel. For example, cat = cab-at; dog = dab-og; dinner = dab-inner; that = thab-at.

'POLISH COUNT' also uses the first vowel of each word. This time you add the sound of 'op' (as in 'stop') before the first vowel, and then pronounce the rest of the word. Here's how it works: desk = dop-esk; pencil = pop-encil; gum = gop-um.

Kids in Japan have a language all their own, too. They place the letter 'k' after the first vowel, repeat the same vowel after the 'k', and then pronounce the rest of the word. Here's an example of how that would work in English:

paper = pa + k + a + per = pay-kay-per; note = no-kote.

Carny

This slang is often used on the carnival or fair grounds when a member of the troupe wants to say something so that it can't be understood by the 'townies' – the people from the town where they're appearing.

Once again you use the first vowel of each word, but this

time you add the two sounds of 'ee-ess' before that vowel. For example, let's use the word 'book'. Start with the sound of 'b', add 'ee-ess', and then pronounce the rest of the word. It ends up 'bee-ess-ook'. Here are some other examples:

street = stree-ess-eet; wall = wee-ess-all;

shop = shee-ess-op.

It's really confusing when you mix 'Carny' with regular English, using Carny just for the important words. Suppose you wanted to say, 'I'm going to see John's mum about the show.' By mixing the two languages and leaving out a couple of unimportant words you have the following mind-boggling sounds:

'I'm going to Jee-ess-ohns mee-ess-ums about the shee-ess-ow.'

Rhyming Cockney

The same families lived in the East End of London for generations. They were called Cockneys (although no one really knows why), and they developed their own special English accent as well as private language. It's a very entertaining language because its phrases are made up of words that rhyme. However, these phrases have no connection with the words they really mean. The Cockneys invented this language so outsiders – and the police – couldn't tell what they were saying.

In the 1800s many Cockneys got in trouble with the law. Because England needed people to be pioneers, some of these Cockneys were sent to Australia instead of to jail. That's why lots of Australians speak the slang too.

See if you can play with these Cockney phrases in conversations with your friends. (For example, instead of 'boots', you'd say 'daisy roots'.)

church – lean and lurch
drink – tumble down the sink
eyes – mince pies
feet – plates of meat
hands – German bands
hat – titfer (tit for tat)
home – top of Rome
look – butcher's (hook)
mouth – north and south
pub – rub-a-dub-dub
sneeze – bread and cheese
socks – almond rocks
stairs – apples and pears
suit – whistle and flute
tea – Rosy Lee
teeth – Hampstead Heath
thief – tealeaf

Nonsense Naming

You and your gang get together and decide on new names for all of you. In other words, Doris will be known as Bunny, George will be known as Charlie, and Nancy will be known as Cathy. You'll notice we used names that end in 'y' or 'ie' as the code names. This is so they'll be easier to remember.

The next step is to use just initials for places and objects that are frequently used by your group. The library is simply called 'L', and bicycles become 'Bs'.

So, if you want to say, 'Nancy and I are going over to Doris's house on our bicycles for a private party,' it would come out, 'Cathy and I are going to Bunny's H on our Bs for some I-Cs.'

What are I-Cs? Oh, that's *ice creams*.

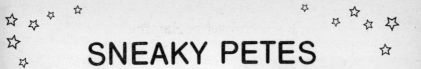

SNEAKY PETES

Sneaky Petes are easy ways to do and remember hard things. Your friends will be dumbfounded as they rack their brains for the answers to these problems, while you have the answers right at hand.

How Many Days?

Thirty days hath September, April, June and November – or is it December? Frankly, I never learned that little rhyme because I knew that when I wanted to work out whether a month had thirty or thirty-one days, I always had that information handy. Not in the palm of my hand but on my knuckles.

You do, too. Hold your right hand, palm down, and make a fist. See how the knuckles are high points like mountains? And between each of the four knuckles is a low point – a valley.

With the index finger of your left hand, touch your first knuckle and call it January. It's a *high* point (a mountain rather than a valley), which tells you that January has the *high* number of days – thirty-one.

Now point to the valley next to that January mountain. Call the valley February. It's lower, so you know that it has a lower number of days (either twenty-eight or twenty-nine).

Next to February is March. A mountain. Thirty-one days again. Then point to the low valley next to March. That's April and, like all low months (except February), April has only thirty days.

And so it goes. As you can see, July lands on a mountain (thirty-one days) and from July you switch to the first knuckle of your left hand for August – which is the first mountain on the left (thirty-one days), followed by September, down in the valley, with thirty days (remember 'thirty days hath September'). And when you show this amazing technique to your friends, I'll bet no one will ever fight with you about whether or not it works – because there you'll be, standing in front of them with your hand already in a fist!

Nines at Your Fingertips

Did you know that you can multiply by nine on your fingers?

Hold your two hands in front of you, thumbs facing one another. If you want to work out what 1 times 9 equals, bend down the little finger of your left hand. What's left is the answer: 1 times 9 equals 9 – and there are nine fingers sticking up.

For 2 times 9, bend down your left ring finger only. Again, what's left is the answer. On one side of that bent ring finger is a 1, on the other, an 8. So 2 times 9 equals 1 and 8 – 18.

Work out 3 times 9 by bending down only your left middle finger. To the left of that bent finger are 2 fingers sticking up, to the right, 7. So your answer is 27. That means that 3 times 9 equals 27. Is that right? Yes, that's right!

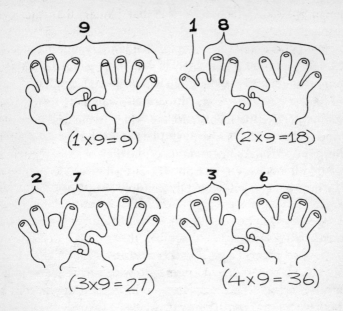

$(1 \times 9 = 9)$

$(2 \times 9 = 18)$

$(3 \times 9 = 27)$

$(4 \times 9 = 36)$

I guess you can work the rest of it out, but it's too amazing for me to stop now! Here's 4 times 9: bend only the left index finger down. That leaves 3 fingers sticking up to the left; 6 to the left – 36! (Which is what you get when you multiply 4 times 9, of course!)

A word of warning: if you do this during a test in school, your teacher will either think you've gone a bit strange or that you are signalling to a friend, so I suggest that you practise well in advance and work it out with your fingers in your lap.

The '11 Times' Short Cut

Here's the shortest short cut to multiplying any two-digit number by 11. If the two-digit number is a low one, add the two digits and plop the sum in the middle. (So, to multiply 45 by 11, just add the 4 and the 5. That gives you 9. Put the nine in the middle between the 4 and the 5, and you have the answer, 495.)

When the sum of the two digits is 10 or more (as it will be if you are multiplying, say, 85 by 11) here's what you do: add the two digits together in the same way (8 and 5 is 13). Now add the first digit of the sum of those two numbers to the first number. (Take the 1 of the 13 and add it to the first number, which is the 8. That gives you 9.) Then take the second digit of that sum (13 is the sum, and the second digit of 13 is 3), put it in the middle, between the 9 and the 5. That gives 935, which is exactly what you get when you multiply 85 by 11.